# OUR BILL OF RIGHTS

# THE RIGHT TO BEAR ARMS

## A LOOK AT THE SECOND AMENDMENT

### DAVID LOUIS

PowerKiDS press™

NEW YORK

Published in 2019 by The Rosen Publishing Group, Inc.
29 East 21st Street, New York, NY 10010

Editor: Sharon Gleason
Book Design: Rachel Rising

Photo Credits: Cover Kzenon/Shutterstock.com; Cover, pp. 1, 3, 4, 6, 8, 9, 10, 11, 12, 14, 15, 16, 17, 18, 19, 20, 22, 23, 24, 25, 26, 27, 28, 29, 30, 31, 32 Mad Dog/Shutterstock.com; Cover, pp. 1, 3, 4, 6, 8, 9, 10, 11, 12, 14, 15, 16, 17, 18, 19, 20, 22, 23, 24, 25, 26, 27, 28, 29, 30, 31, 32 (background) Flas100/Shutterstock.com; pp. 4, 18 (arrow) Forest Foxy/Shutterstock.com; p. 5 Onur ERSIN/Shutterstock.com; p. 7 Gregory Johnston/Shutterstock.com; p. 9 Dave Weaver/Shutterstock.com; p. 10 Robert Przybysz/Shutterstock.com; p. 11 sirtravelalot/Shutterstock.com; p. 13 Charles Knowles/Shutterstock.com; p. 15 (insert) https://commons.wikimedia.org/wiki/File:Gatling_gun_1865.jpg; p. 15 Geoff Brightling/Dorling Kindersley/Getty Images; p. 16 Bettmann/Contributor/Getty Images; pp. 17, 19 Hulton Archive/Staff/Getty Images; p. 20 William Warren/SuperStock/Getty Images; p. 21 Popperfoto/Contributor/Getty Images; p. 23 JIM WATSON/Staff/Getty Images; p. 25 Keith Homan/Shutterstock.com; p. 26 EMMANUEL DUNAND/AFP/Getty Images; p. 27 Andrey_Popov/Shutterstock.com; p. 29 Vera Larina/Shutterstock.com; p. 30 Militarist/Shutterstock.com.

Library of Congress Cataloging-in-Publication Data

Names: Louis, David, author.
Title: The right to bear arms : a look at the Second Amendment / David Louis.
Description: New York : PowerKids Press, [2019] | Series: Our Bill of Rights
    | Includes index.
Identifiers: LCCN 2018020444| ISBN 9781538342947 (library bound) | ISBN
    9781538342923 (pbk.) | ISBN 9781538342930 (6 pack)
Subjects: LCSH: Firearms--Law and legislation--United States--Juvenile
    literature. | United States. Constitution. 2nd Amendment--Juvenile
    literature. | Gun control--United States--Juvenile literature.
Classification: LCC KF3941 .H64 2019 | DDC 344.7305/33--dc23
LC record available at https://lccn.loc.gov/2018020444

Manufactured in the United States of America

CPSIA Compliance Information: Batch #CWPK19 For further information contact Rosen Publishing, New York, New York at 1-800-237-9932.

# CONTENTS

# WE THE PEOPLE

In 1788, the new United States ratified, or approved, the U.S. Constitution. With its opening three words—"We the People"—the Constitution shows how the nation will be governed by its citizens and for its citizens. The Constitution lays out the supreme laws and framework of the U.S. government. It also describes the basic rights of all its citizens.

However, many states and citizens wanted further promises that the government would respect the rights of the people. Congress approved a list of possible amendments, or changes, in 1789 and sent them to the states, which ratified 10 of them. These amendments are the Bill of Rights. Some amendments protect the personal rights of citizens. Other amendments put limits on the government's power. The Second Amendment would set the stage for **debate** that's lasted for more than 200 years.

The Bill of Rights was added to the Constitution to protect the freedom and individual rights of Americans.

# AN IMPORTANT DEBATE

"A well regulated **Militia**, being necessary to the security of a free State, the right of the people to keep and bear Arms, shall not be **infringed**."

People have debated the meaning of the 27 words of the Second Amendment for more than 200 years. It's an argument that shows no sign of slowing anytime soon. Today, the Second Amendment is debated in the classroom and in the courtroom. It's debated on television and radio. It's debated in the streets with protests and counterprotests.

The arguments about the Second Amendment aren't simple. Some people believe all citizens should be able to have any sort of gun with few regulations. Some people believe there should be many controls (or complete bans) on all guns. Many people are somewhere in the middle.

## KNOW YOUR RIGHTS!

It's been reported that the number of guns owned by people in the United States was 310 million as of 2009, and the number is growing.

The debate over the meaning of the Second Amendment has led to deep divides among Americans. People have strong feelings about the issue.

# A WELL-REGULATED MILITIA

It was only a few years after the American Revolution when the Founding Fathers crafted the U.S. Constitution and Bill of Rights. Many feared the British or another foreign power could still overthrow the young nation.

During the Revolution, militias played a part in defeating the powerful British army. Militias were made up of men from the 13 colonies. They took up arms, trained quickly, and marched into battle against the occupying forces from England. Armed with muskets, rifles, pistols, and other simple **firearms**, militias helped win the Revolutionary War and earn America's freedom.

The Second Amendment, written shortly after the war, acknowledges the militias. The first part of the amendment reads, "A well regulated Militia, being necessary to the security of a free State." The Founding Fathers believed that an armed militia could protect U.S. citizens. But did their intent for the Second Amendment stop with militias? Or was the right to own guns granted to all citizens?

# THE NATIONAL GUARD

In 1792, Congress passed the Militia Acts, requiring every "able-bodied free white citizen" to join their local militia. Today, the National Guard acts as the reserve system of America's military with units that date back to 1636.

Each state's National Guard is commanded by its state's governor, who can call on the troops in times of emergency. The president can also call the soldiers to duty.

# TO KEEP AND BEAR ARMS

The Bill of Rights explains the powers of government and the rights of individuals. But questions quickly emerged about personal rights and the role of government. Where do personal rights begin and where do they end? What role should government play in citizens' personal freedoms?

Some people believe the Second Amendment only applies to organizations meant to protect the public, such as the police. Others believe it applies to all citizens, as long as they follow the laws.

The Second Amendment clause "the right of the people to keep and bear Arms, shall not be infringed" raises the question of collective rights and individual rights. Collective rights supporters say this key phrase only allows militias or other military forces to possess and use firearms to protect the general public. Individual rights supporters say this phrase shows that it's the right of all citizens to own guns, as long as they're used for legal purposes such as self-defense or hunting. This phrase of the Second Amendment clearly gives people the right to keep and bear arms. But for whom were these rights intended?

# SHALL NOT BE INFRINGED

It took months for enough states to ratify the Constitution. Many people argued about the powers of government and the rights of citizens. On one side, the Federalists believed in a strong central government, one that could better protect the young nation. Meanwhile, the anti-Federalists wanted more power to remain with states and local governments. Among other things, they were concerned the central government would have too much military power.

The Founding Fathers had fundamental differences of opinion on the role of government and individual rights. However, both the Federalists and anti-Federalists agreed at the time that no government should have the power to infringe personal rights such as the right to keep and bear arms.

## KNOW YOUR RIGHTS!

James Madison wrote the original Bill of Rights. He modeled the Second Amendment after a statement in a similar Bill of Rights in his home state of Virginia.

When the Founding Fathers were creating the Constitution, the Federalists and the anti-Federalists agreed on some things, but they disagreed on many others.

# THE WAY OF THE GUN

Whatever the authors of the Second Amendment intended, the Founding Fathers probably never imagined the changes America would go through. Guns would play an important role in shaping the new nation.

During the 1800s, U.S. citizens were moving west into the frontier. Like the colonists before them, settlers relied on firearms for hunting and protection in a sometimes dangerous land. In 1835, gunmaker Samuel Colt unveiled his classic revolver. The Colt revolver would become the preferred firearm of both lawmen and criminals of the Wild West. The Civil War from 1861 to 1865 saw big developments in gun **technology**, too, making the weapons more reliable, easier to use, and more powerful than ever before.

## LOSING OUR LEADERS

Following the Civil War, three presidents were **assassinated** with guns. President Abraham Lincoln was killed in 1865, followed by presidents James Garfield (1881) and William McKinley (1901).

# THE GATLING GUN

The Civil War helped usher in a new age of firearms with the Gatling gun. This large machine gun could fire up to 1,000 rounds of ammunition, or bullets, per minute. The Gatling gun was the most powerful and destructive weapon of its time.

The 1800s saw major advances in firearms technology. The Colt revolver was used by lawmen and criminals alike.

# EARLY GUN CONTROL

By the 1920s, gun culture was taking hold in America. Guns became a part of life for criminals in big cities such as Chicago and New York. Rapid-fire submachine guns, called tommy guns, allowed gangs to leave a bloody trail of terror and crime across the United States.

A rise in violent crimes led to the federal government's first gun-control laws, setting the stage for the debate over the Second Amendment in the following years.

**TOMMY GUN**

With crime out of control, President Franklin D. Roosevelt and Congress put in place the nation's first major gun-control laws. These laws, they hoped, would stop the bloodshed. The National Firearms Act of 1934 taxed the manufacture, sale, and transport of some guns. It also required owners of those guns to register them. In 1938, the Federal Firearms Act required gun dealers to get a license and keep records. It also limited gun ownership for those who'd been convicted of certain crimes.

Gun **advocates** began to push back. They feared these laws infringed on personal rights to own guns.

# IN THE COURTS

The Second Amendment has a long history in the courts. Some cases even landed in the Supreme Court, the highest court in the nation. The first of these court cases was *United States v. Cruikshank* (1876). Just a few years before, the 14th Amendment had been added to the Constitution, granting equal rights to newly freed slaves. However, organizations such as the **Ku Klux Klan** tried to keep freed slaves from their rights, such as the right to assemble or to own a gun.

In 1939, in *United States v. Miller*, the Supreme Court agreed that the Second Amendment doesn't protect an individual's right to own any gun. This decision would lay the groundwork for the fierce Second Amendment debates that rage to this day.

Even after the ratification of the 14th Amendment, many white Americans believed freed slaves shouldn't have equal rights.

# THE COLFAX MASSACRE

The debate over the 14th Amendment boiled over during the bitter time following the Civil War. On April 13, 1873, in Colfax, Louisiana, a group of white people killed more than 100 African Americans who had gathered at the state capitol. Following the **massacre**, some of the white people were arrested and charged with **conspiring** to keep others from their constitutional rights. The case (*United States v. Cruikshank*) went to the Supreme Court, which stated that the law only applied to state actions, not the actions of individuals such as the attackers—and that the Constitution didn't grant individuals (referring to the African Americans in this case) the right to bear arms.

# A CHANGING SOCIETY

By the 1960s, America was experiencing many changes. The Vietnam War and the fight for civil rights divided the nation. Arguments over the Second Amendment became louder, too, after a string of killings and assassinations. In 1966, a student at the University of Texas used a high-powered rifle to kill 14 people at the school. President John F. Kennedy, civil rights leader Martin Luther King Jr., and presidential candidate Robert F. Kennedy were all assassinated by people using guns.

These events led to the passage of the Gun Control Act of 1968, which placed even more restrictions on gun owners.

Law enforcement officials were heavily armed during protests against the Vietnam War in the 1960s.

# GUN CONTROL GAINS STRENGTH

With increasing gun violence across the country during the 1970s, the push for even more gun control grew stronger. Some gun-control advocates believe that fewer firearms will greatly reduce gun-related crimes. Some supporters of gun control want more regulations that limit the people who can own or possess a gun.

Some gun-control advocates support laws such as limiting access to guns for people with mental illness or those convicted of violent crimes. Other supporters of gun control want to ban assault-style rifles or powerful ammunition normally reserved for military use. These measures, some gun-control advocates believe, would reduce gun-related violence in the United States.

## KNOW YOUR RIGHTS!

Thanks to a sharp rise in gun violence, Congress banned the manufacture and sale of assault rifles in 1994. The ban expired in 2004.

# THE BRADY BILL

On the afternoon of March 30, 1981, a gunman shot President Ronald Reagan in an assassination attempt. The gunman also shot three others, including press secretary Jim Brady. All four men survived the shooting, but Brady was left partly **paralyzed**. Brady became a champion of gun control. A gun-control measure called the Brady Bill was signed into law in 1993 and would become a milestone in the fight over the Second Amendment. The new law required gun dealers to run background checks on people who wanted to buy guns.

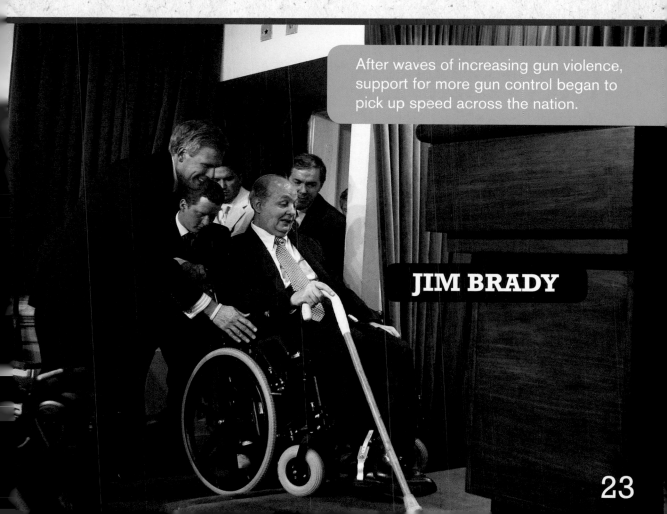

After waves of increasing gun violence, support for more gun control began to pick up speed across the nation.

**JIM BRADY**

# PUSHBACK

Opposing the supporters of gun control are gun-rights advocates who believe that it's a constitutional right to own guns, a right that "shall not be infringed" upon by the government. The words of the Second Amendment, they argue, clearly state that it's the right of every American to own a firearm.

Many gun-rights advocates believe any American should be allowed to own and use a gun, as long as the firearm is used in a safe and legal manner. Guns may be used for protection, for hunting, or for recreation. Many gun-rights advocates also point to the fact that firearms protected our forefathers from **oppressive** governments. Guns, they say, are part of the fabric of American freedom. Firearms, after all, helped win America's freedom from the British during the American Revolution.

In 1986, the Firearm Owners' Protection Act was passed. It increased the rights of gun owners while still trying to maintain public safety.

# THE NATIONAL RIFLE ASSOCIATION

Gun-rights advocates' most powerful **ally** is the National Rifle Association (NRA). Founded in 1871 as a way to "promote and encourage rifle shooting," the NRA is now a political force with great influence in state and federal governments. Supporters of the NRA say the organization plays a vital role in advocating for responsible gun ownership. Others feel the NRA has too much political power and does little to help solve the problems of gun violence in America.

Even with the pushback from gun-control advocates, gun ownership has skyrocketed in recent years.

# WEAPONS OF MURDER

There have been a number of deadly school shootings and other massacres at places such as shopping malls and movie theaters in recent years. In some ways, these events have deepened the divide between gun-rights advocates and those who support gun control.

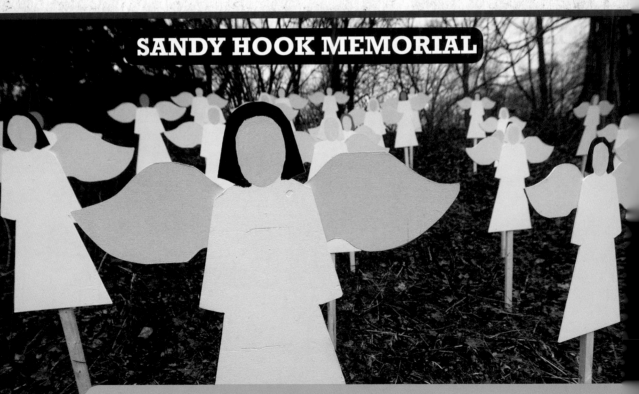

## SANDY HOOK MEMORIAL

On December 14, 2012, a gunman killed 20 students and six teachers in an elementary school in Neweton, Connecticut. These wooden angels were set up in a nearby location as a memorial.

The increase in school shootings has sparked a fierce debate over armed teachers in schools.

Gun-rights advocates often argue that these sites need more armed protection. Some believe that arming teachers would help to prevent school shootings. Arming and training people to use guns, they say, is one way to reduce the number of mass killings.

Many gun-control advocates believe it's too easy to purchase deadly weapons in the United States. Many of these weapons, such as powerful assault rifles, aren't used for hunting or personal protection. These weapons, they say, are only used to commit violent crimes.

# RIGHT TO SELF-DEFENSE

Some new gun-rights laws have pushed the limits of debate over the Second Amendment. Gun-rights advocates argue that these laws protect the basic rights of Americans—just as the Founding Fathers intended. Gun-control advocates, however, suggest these laws only increase gun violence by making it easier to possess and use firearms.

All the U.S. states have "concealed carry" laws that allow gun owners to carry a hidden firearm. Gun-rights advocates believe these are necessary laws that help reduce crime and provide greater freedom for personal protection. Gun-control supporters say laws such as these only increase the chance of conflict and accidents.

## KNOW YOUR RIGHTS!

Forty-two states require people to have a concealed-carry permit (known as a CCW permit). In order to get a CCW permit, gun owners must complete several hours of training on gun safety and the law.

# SHOOTING SPORTS AND YOUTH

Shooting sports are gaining popularity across the nation, especially with the younger generation. Shooting clubs offer a variety of events and competitions. These clubs promote responsible gun ownership while providing a range of different shooting types, from target shooting to long-range competitions.

Some states have "stand-your-ground" laws that give people the right to use force, even deadly force, in a place where they have a right to be. Supporters say these laws allow people to use firearms to protect themselves when their life is threatened. Others argue this type of law allows gun owners to use firearms when they aren't needed and encourages violence.

Some recent laws have only deepened the divide between gun-rights and gun-control advocates.

# THE DEBATE RAGES ON

The debate over the Second Amendment shows no sign of slowing down. Both sides of the debate are loyal to their beliefs. Each side is armed with facts and figures to support their beliefs. Every week, it seems, current events help fuel the debate for or against the Second Amendment.

Who's right? Who's wrong? That's a matter of opinion. However, the ongoing debate over the Second Amendment points to the wisdom the Founding Fathers showed more than two centuries ago. The Constitution and the Bill of Rights have stood the test of time, ensuring rights to all Americans. The First Amendment— the right to free speech—promises that the debate over the Second Amendment isn't going to end anytime soon.

# GLOSSARY

**advocate:** A person who argues for or supports a cause or policy, or to support or argue for a cause or policy.

**ally:** One of two or more people or groups who work together.

**assassinate:** The killing of a public figure, often for political reasons.

**conspire:** To secretly plan to do something unlawful.

**debate:** A discussion in which people express different opinions, or to discuss different opinions about something.

**firearm:** A gun.

**infringe:** To wrongly limit or take away.

**Ku Klux Klan:** An American hate group made up of white people opposed to people of other groups.

**massacre:** The violent killing of many people.

**militia:** A group of people who are not an official part of the armed forces of a country but are trained like soldiers.

**oppressive:** Unjustly harsh or severe.

**paralyzed:** Unable to move.

**technology:** A method that uses science to solve problems and the tools used to solve those problems.

# INDEX

# WEBSITES

Due to the changing nature of Internet links, PowerKids Press has developed an online list of websites related to the subject of this book. This site is updated regularly. Please use this link to access the list: www.powerkidslinks.com/obor/second